SCHOOLHOUSE
APPLIQUÉ

Reverse techniques and more...

**CHARLOTTE
PATERA**

C&T PUBLISHING

Schoolhouse Appliqué: Reverse techniques and more...
©1995 Charlotte Patera

Photographer (unless otherwise noted): Tom Yarish
Editor: Louise Owens Townsend
Technical Editor: Sally Lanzarotti
Design & Art Director: Rose Sheifer

Published by C&T Publishing, P.O. Box 1456, Lafayette, California 94549

ISBN: 0-914881-99-X

Library of Congress Cataloging-in-Publication Data

Patera, Charlotte, 1927–
    Schoolhouse appliqué : reverse techniques and more... / by Charlotte Patera.
        p.   cm.
    ISBN 0-914881-99-X
    1. Appliqué—Patterns.   2. Quilting—Patterns.   3. School buildings in art.
  I. Title.
TT779.P378   1995
746.44'5—dc20   95–14966
                                                                    CIP

You will find that photocopy shops are becoming more scrupulous about copying from published material. Many quilters and quilting teachers have experienced the heartbreak of seeing obvious adaptations of their original ideas at quilt exhibitions winning awards and drawing glowing comments from viewers with no credit to themselves. Seeing a quilt work that was inspired from one's design is a mixed blessing. It is a delight to see that someone enjoyed the design, tried it in new colors, sizes, and added some personal touches obtaining obvious pleasure in so doing. It is also disturbing to see that although appropriate credit went to the maker, none went to the originator. More serious is the publication, marketing, and teaching of "borrowed" ideas, without permission. Remember to give credit where it is due, and to ask permission before using someone else's idea for commercial purposes.

We have made every attempt to properly credit the trademarks and brand names of the items mentioned in this book. We apologize to any companies that have been listed incorrectly, and we would appreciate hearing from you.

The Apple logo is a trademark of Apple Computer, Inc.
Mettler is a brand name of Arova Mettler AG.

Printed in Hong Kong   10 9 8 7 6 5 4 3 2 1

B

Table of Contents

DEDICATION

To Charlie and our

Home Sweet Home.
1995.
13½" x 17".
Hand quilted.
(Photo by Steve Buckley)

ACKNOWLEDGMENTS

My students who asked, "Is there a book on this?"
Dena Canty, Bara Joses, Jeanne and Gordon Rosenberry for lending their quilts
Susan Bradford for permission to show the Sun Valley School quilt
Rindy Evans for checking my manuscript
Tom Yarish for his photography
Charles Patera for free use of his computer as he often asked, "Are you still working on that house?"
Sally Lanzarotti and Louise Townsend for their technical and copy editing
Rose Sheifer for designing this book
Diane Pedersen and Marta Kokron for design production
Todd Hensley and Tony Hensley, owners of C&T Publishing, who published this book

One day I realized that I had seldom seen a Schoolhouse quilt I didn't like. Every example I see gives me a little feeling of delight. Traditionally they are pieced but the basic Schoolhouse is a natural for easy appliqué. Some call them "House" quilts and some call them "Schoolhouse" quilts. I do not know of any historical differentiation between the two, but I prefer the term Schoolhouse quilts.

I made my first Schoolhouse quilt in 1986, and one quilt led to another. Although the concept for a book came in 1988, I didn't get to pursue the project in depth until 1993. After I started to make Schoolhouse quilts, it occurred to me that this would be an easy pattern to use to teach beginners the joys of both appliqué and reverse appliqué. Reverse appliqué is often thought of as exotic, too complex to understand, or overly ambitious. Some books devote only a sentence or a brief paragraph to the subject, as though it is a necessary evil to be alluded to and ignored. The idea is perpetuated in many books, articles and lectures, often with the assurance that it is "difficult." Reverse appliqué is almost always associated

Appliqué (Image in Positive)

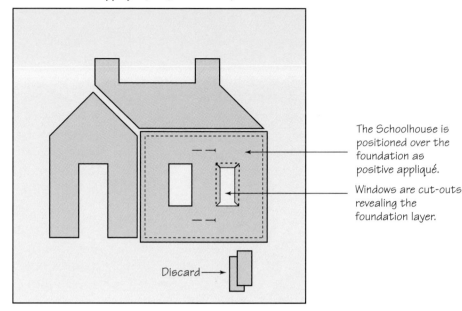

The Schoolhouse is positioned over the foundation as positive appliqué.

Windows are cut-outs revealing the foundation layer.

Discard →

with molas, a misinterpretation made by many needleworkers.

Most of the molas, made by the Kuna Indians of the San Blas Islands in Panama, are made with repeated outlines in complicated combinations of both negative and positive appliqué. Reverse appliqué (a technique) and mola work (a cultural discipline) are frequently described as being worked with many layers and cut from the top layer down. I have never seen this technique in quilt shows or other displays of needlework. I wonder "Does anyone actually do that?" and "Why is it always described that way?" The Kuna Indians would be amused if they knew how their work was perceived. They work from the foundation up, and fabric is very seldom cut away and removed. When a piece is removed in one of their many methods, there is always a very detailed replacement for the cut-away discard.

Reverse appliqué is almost a misnomer because the method is not really different from regular appliqué. I often

Reverse Appliqué. (Image in Negative)

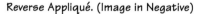

The Schoolhouse is visible as a cut-out in the top or appliqué layer. The Schoolhouse is the underneath fabric revealed through the cut-out as negative appliqué.

Windows are cut from the discarded top layer while it is still in position, pinned in place, and appliquéd over the underneath layer.

Discard

use the terms "positive appliqué" and "negative appliqué" to distinguish between the two results that can be achieved with the same method. But the term "reverse appliqué" seems unalterable.

(Negative) reverse appliqué is often simpler and easier than (positive) direct appliqué, which is why I do more of it than direct appliqué. The Schoolhouse pattern provides a simple way to teach reverse appliqué to convince doubters that it is not so "foreign" after all. In this book, you will notice more examples of reverse appliqué than appliqué because it is the way I prefer to work most of the time.

You may notice that the basic pattern I use has changed several times. The first schoolhouse had three windows. After that, I changed one window to

a door. On one quilt, I repositioned a chimney. In my early quilts, I used only solid fabrics. Eventually, I started to silkscreen my own fabrics to achieve a more dynamic look. Finally, when stimulating prints began to appear on the market, I changed my approach to quiltmaking. I began to use the prints that were unlike any previously available for quilters.

I like the Schoolhouse block for several reasons. It is a good basic symbol. Like a good logo, it is simple and bold with a strong impact. It symbolizes the home, a place of warmth, comfort, and security

both emotional and physical. It can also symbolize a comfortable, secure space, not necessarily a building but a good friend, a circle of supportive friends or relatives, a particular situation or role in life in which one feels good or real—when you feel glad that you are "you!"

With so many disasters occurring today, many of us are very grateful that we have not had to undergo the loss of our homes through fire, floods, hurricanes, and earthquakes as so many others have. We also feel much empathy for the unfortunate people who have been devastated by these catastrophes. It makes our secure homes more precious to us and reminds us of how easily we could lose them. The possibility of such a loss is a realistic concern. I tried to depict this fear in the small quilt on page 45.

I once heard that in a study of drawings by children around the world, whether they lived in apartments, yurts, hogans, thatched huts, palaces, or modern ranch houses, they always draw a house as a square with a peaked roof, chimney, doorway, and windows. It is a universal symbol.

One time a woman told me she had made a study of old schoolhouses and that after photographing at least 200 of them, declared that not one had two chimneys. What could I say? Designers often take liberties with realism. Perhaps the woman who first designed a Schoolhouse block for her quilt felt that it balanced better with two chimneys. Or do you like one chimney?

I hope this book will give readers some ideas for working with the Schoolhouse pattern and that they will experiment with many fabrics and different ways of using it.

CHAPTER ONE

Materials and Supplies

FABRIC

The best fabric for appliqué is a lightweight cotton. I like 100% cotton with a very fine weave because it is the easiest to use. It behaves when you fold it under, and it creases well with finger pressing. You may want to use a cotton/polyester blend sometimes, but it tends to have a mind of its own, especially in the hands of a beginner.

I like cotton because it feels good and looks good. Most quilters insist on it. Pima cotton is the treasure of cotton for appliqué when you can find it. While you are shopping in the stores, you will find some cottons that are coarser and heavier than others. Try to choose the finer ones. The finer the cotton weave, the less bulk to contend with when folding under corners. Coarser weaves arc good for the underlayer or foundation pieces that do not have to be folded and manipulated.

Previously, I worked only with solid colors because they produced the crisp graphic effect that I preferred with less effort. I liked a strong contrast between colors. Prints may not offer this contrast unless you have a very practiced and discerning eye. When I began working with prints, I silk-screened my own because I could not find many that I liked. Now there are more exciting prints being offered than ever before. Well-known quilters are designing irresistible prints for quilters, which I find myself choosing over solids. Use solids or prints, or combine them as you prefer.

I offer a warning with light-colored fabric: Darker colors often show through so that folded-under edges of a lighter color are very visible over a dark color. Also, I recommend that you pre-wash fabrics to minimize future shrinking and fading.

THREAD

I have no preference in thread types for hand stitching. The important thing is that the thread's color match the top appliqué piece being sewn to the underneath piece. Sometimes it is impossible to match the color perfectly. When I cannot match it, I think that a slightly darker shade shows less than a slightly lighter one with medium and dark colors; use a lighter shade for light colors. Thread used in the sewing machine requires careful selection, but threads for hand sewing are not as temperamental. Mettler machine embroidery thread is excellent because it is thin. Stitches will be almost invisible. Machine embroidery thread should be used in short lengths in handwork—no longer than 18"—because it shreds easily if it travels through the fabric too often.

SCISSORS

This is the most important tool for this style of appliqué. Small embroidery scissors with very fine sharp points are essential. For reverse appliqué or cut-outs, the point can be used to stab and lift the upper fabric away from the underneath fabric for cutting. It is also necessary to cut right into the inner points. Students sometimes find difficulty and frustration if they cannot cut with the points of the scissors they use. Dull or blunt points on your scissors will cause endless anxiety.

PINS

Simple straight silk pins, which are thinner than others, work well. I like to use the longer ones (1¼"). Pins that have bead heads or other fancy shapes get in the way. Only a few pins are needed for any piece in this book.

NEEDLES

I also like thin needles, preferably size 11 or 12 sharps, but they are sometimes hard to thread. I also like crewel needles, which are thin, because they have larger eyes for threading. Size 10 is the thinnest I can find in crewel needles. Milliner's straw needles are excellent, though some bend quickly.

NEEDLE THREADER

This is helpful when it is troublesome to thread a fine needle or when the thread gets limp with use and has to be re-threaded.

NEEDLE SAFE

A needle safe or needle keeper is a very thin case with a magnetic interior that keeps needles in place. A needle threader will also fit inside of it.

DRESSMAKER'S TRACING CARBON PAPER

Use this paper for transferring a design to the appliqué fabric. Place it between the paper pattern and the fabric, colored side down on the fabric on a table. It comes with several colors in a package. Choose a color that contrasts with your fabric so you can see it. Some are washable, but they are lighter in color and do not always make a good clear image. I usually use the type that is not washable, then fold the traced line under as I work so it will not be seen.

TRACING WHEEL

This is used to trace paper patterns onto fabric with the carbon paper. Some are serrated and produce a dotted line when rolling it along the edge of a shape. Some are not, producing a solid line. The serrated ones wear out the paper pattern sooner but make a visible yet less prominent line.

PENCILS

A hard pencil (4H or 6H) may be used for tracing instead of the tracing wheel especially when the detail is too small to trace with the wheel. An ordinary writing pencil is handy for touching up traced lines that may start rubbing off before they are stitched. A sharp white pencil is useful for touching up white lines traced on darker fabrics.

PENCIL SHARPENER

It is essential to keep your pencil point sharp so that you are able to draw a fine accurate line. Turn-ing the traced line under to get it out of sight is easier when it is very thin. An electric pencil sharpener for studio use is best but a small battery-operated one is good for class use.

PENS

Permanent-ink fine-point pens for marking are being sold in quilting shops now. These are excellent and will keep a fine line. Do not use one that will bleed into the fabric.

ROTARY CUTTER, CUTTING MAT, AND CUTTING RULER

Most quilters have found these tools a necessity. Use them after you have finished your appliqué to cut an accurate, square block for seaming.

LIGHT BOX (OPTIONAL)

A light box is an excellent way to trace without using tracing carbon paper. It provides a translucent tracing surface over a light. Professional ones are very expensive but there are less expensive versions available for quilters. A light box enables you to see the pattern underneath the fabric.

LAP DESK (OPTIONAL)

Since I like to work on a flat surface like a table, a lap desk provides the same convenience while sitting anywhere. It is a piece of essential equipment for me. I like to keep the appliqué piece flat on the surface as I work, finger pressing and stitching long straight edges, then picking up the work when necessary.

CHAPTER TWO

Techniques

SIZING

You may want to change the size of the patterns in this book. The patterns may be taken to a photocopy machine and reduced or enlarged.

A pocket calculator comes in handy at the copy shop or to use before you go. Divide the size you want by the size you have. Change the resulting decimal figure to the closest percent and set the machine at that number. Example: Your pattern measures 7", and you want to reduce it to 6". Divide 6 by 7. The calculator results in 0.8571428. Set the copy machine for 86%. If you want to enlarge the 7" pattern to 8", divide 8 by 7. The calculator results in 1.1428571. Set the machine for 114%.

If you want to change the size to a precise but awkward fraction such as $4\frac{5}{16}$", which is difficult to use on a calculator, I suggest using a metric ruler to measure. Change the fraction size to millimeters: $4\frac{5}{16}$" equals 109mm on a metric ruler; 7" equals 178mm; divide 109 by 178. The result is 0.6123595 or 61%.

If the copy machine does not reduce to a size as small as you wish, simply make a reduction and reduce the reduction. The patterns in this book are given at a size that is comfortable to sew. In designing your own quilts you may want to try other sizes.

TRACING PREPARATION

When tracing your pattern, be sure to position it properly so that there is ample fabric around the final piece for finishing it off as you desire. Know exactly what you are going to do with it. Allow enough space around the perimeter of the design so that you can seam it to other pieces for making a quilt, pillow, garment or wall hanging. If you plan to stretch it for framing, allow plenty of fabric around it so that it can be pulled tight enough. I suggest allowing more than needed for any appliqué. Make your piece at least ½" larger than the seam line all around to allow for seams plus any drawing up that may occur as you do the appliqué work. Everyone works at a different tension so that the final size can vary. Do the final trimming and marking of a block after the appliqué is completed.

TRACING THE PATTERN

Position the pattern over the appliqué fabric and pin. Place the tracing carbon paper between the pattern and fabric with the carbon side down on the fabric. Always pin the pattern to the fabric and move the tracing paper as needed. Do not attempt to just hold the three pieces in place as it often slips out of position. Pin it so that the piece will remain stable as you trace. Trace over the lines of the pattern with the tracing wheel or hard pencil. Use a ruler for the straight lines if necessary. Check the traced fabric before tracing the whole design to make sure you are getting a visible image. If not, try another color of carbon paper or try bearing down harder.

If you have a light box, tracing carbon is not needed. You can also use a window in the daytime to trace. Tape the fabric over the pattern on the glass. Use a sharp pencil or one of the fine permanent-ink pens to trace. Make a firm continuous line rather than one made up of short strokes. If your fabric is light enough in color, you can place it over the pattern and see the image through it, eliminating the need for the carbon paper.

Sometimes you will need to trace the pattern in a reversed position, so the schoolhouse faces the other direction. Simply flip the pattern over when

Tracing With Carbon Paper

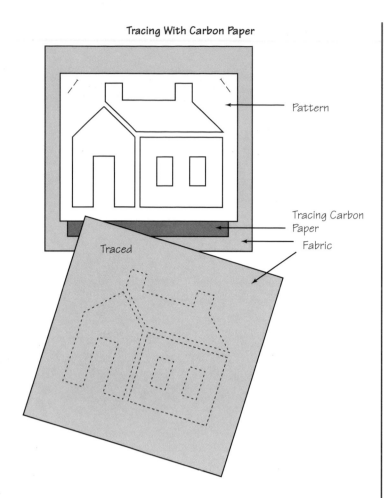

Pattern

Tracing Carbon Paper

Fabric

Traced

tracing. If the pattern has been used before, indentations will be on the reverse side that can be clearly seen, if not, trace over the design once to indent a visible image on the back of it. A light box or a window will show the design from either side.

PINNING

Very few pins are necessary. The patterns in this book are small enough to require no more than four or five on one piece of work. You may prefer to use a few basting stitches instead of pins to secure the pieces together.

I often have some students who feel it is necessary to cut and fold a length of edge under and pin it with many pins close together. This is likely because they have always precut the appliqué and turned under all of the edges before starting the work. So many pins are unnecessary. They get in the way, and the thread gets caught on them. Learn to cut only a little, fold and stitch it under as you work, finger press, and hold it with your thumb. You do not need to have more than an inch or two turned under when you are stitching. Eventually, you may find no necessity to pin the edge under first.

Some appliquérs feel it is essential to precut a design and to use templates to iron the edge under before sewing it under. This approach enables the worker to see the design as it will look when it is finished. I prefer to eliminate any preliminary work and to start stitching as soon as possible. The way I appliqué is based on the principle that if it is not cut it will not travel out of position. When you precut a whole design, loose pieces shift and handling may fray the edges. Cut as you work. I hope this book will give you some inspiration to try this method that may be faster, while achieving excellent results.

APPLIQUÉ TECHNIQUE

As stated before, I like to cut as I work. This applies to both appliqué and reverse appliqué. I trace the appliqué, position it with two or three pins, and then start cutting a little at a time. I begin to stitch, pushing the seam allowance under *toward* myself.

Appliquéing Toward Yourself

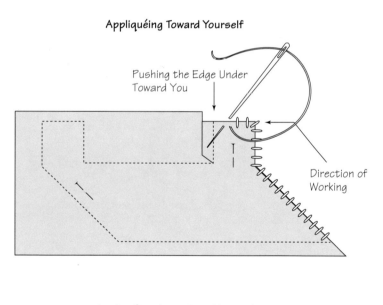

Pushing the Edge Under Toward You

Direction of Working

Appliquéing Away From Yourself

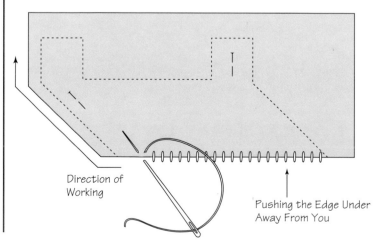

Direction of Working

Pushing the Edge Under Away From You

Some people like to push the edge under *away* from themselves and stitch around the piece in the opposite direction. I have more control if I push the edge toward me. I find that corners and curves are easier to control. Work the way that feels most comfortable to you.

The diagrams here indicate pushing the seam allowance toward yourself, using the right hand.

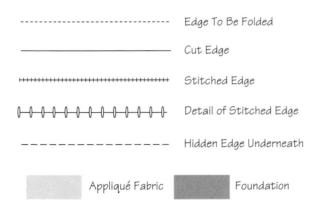

-     Edge To Be Folded

—————————————————————   Cut Edge

++++++++++++++++++++++++++++++++   Stitched Edge

〇〇〇〇〇〇〇〇〇〇〇〇〇〇   Detail of Stitched Edge

— — — — — — — — — —   Hidden Edge Underneath

Appliqué Fabric   Foundation

Step 1. Cut about two inches of the seam allowance approximately ⅛" from the traced line. Knot the thread. Bring it up on the traced line.

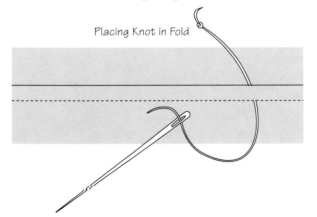

Placing Knot in Fold

Step 2. Use your fingers to fold the allowance under on the traced line. Hold it under with your left forefinger or thumb. I suggest working on a table top or a lap desk.

Folding on Traced Line

Step 3. Insert the needle through the foundation fabric right above the spot where you brought it up on the traced line, and bring it up through both the foundation and the folded-under edge about ⅛" to the left.

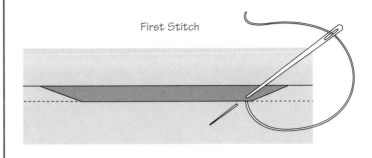

First Stitch

Step 4. Continue stitching in this way, keeping your stitches as even in size and spacing as you can.

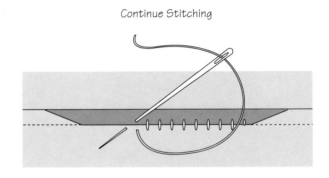

Continue Stitching

Step 5. To work outward corners, trim off a bit of fabric at the tip of a corner.

Outward Corners

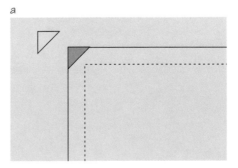

a

Fold under the edge and stitch it to the corner.

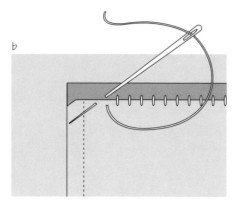

Take a diagonal stitch at the corner and bring the needle back up through the same hole. This will secure the corner. Now it is easy to fold down the adjacent edge while the corner stays in position. Without this extra step, it will wiggle around. Do not try to turn the whole corner under before stitching it one step at a time.

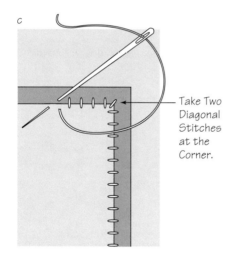

Take Two Diagonal Stitches at the Corner.

Complete the second diagonal stitch (on top of the first) and bring the needle up through the foundation and folded-under edge of the adjacent side.

Step 6. Working the narrow points is a little tricky. You must fold a lot of excess fabric into a smaller space. For that reason, it is necessary to trim off as much of the tip as you can without trimming too much. Trim the tip; then fold under the edge you are working and stitch to the point.

Place a diagonal stitch at the point and bring the needle back up through the same hole. With your scissors, lift up the next edge to be stitched and trim off a bit of the edge that has already been stitched. Do not trim it first because it is easier to fold and stitch it with a larger allowance.

Now trim a bit off of the edge to be stitched. By pushing this edge under with your fingers and needle, it is possible to get it all under without raw threads. Complete the second diagonal stitch (on top of the first) and bring the needle up through the foundation and folded-under edge of the adjacent side.

Stitch that side.

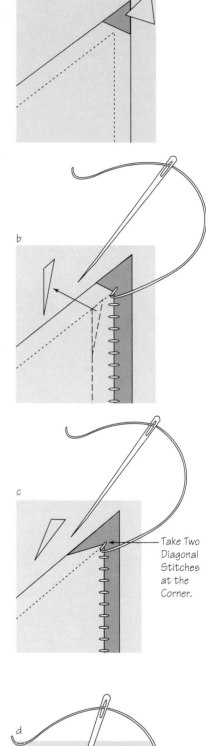

Take Two Diagonal Stitches at the Corner.

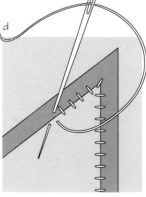

Outward Points, Method 2

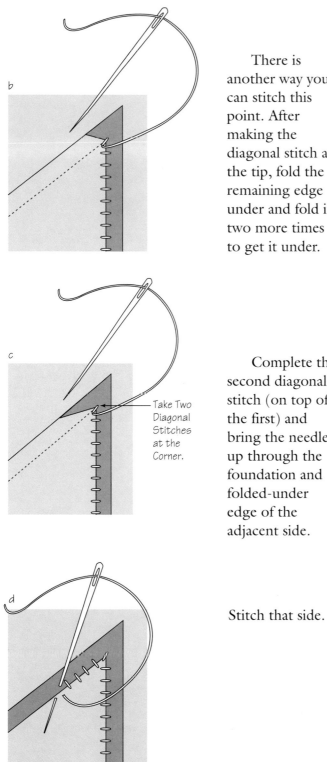

There is another way you can stitch this point. After making the diagonal stitch at the tip, fold the remaining edge under and fold it two more times to get it under.

Complete the second diagonal stitch (on top of the first) and bring the needle up through the foundation and folded-under edge of the adjacent side.

Stitch that side.

Try combining both of these, trimming and folding. After folding with your fingers, use the tip of your needle as a tool to refine the folded-under edge, pushing it in or out as needed. Moisten the corners to help them behave.

Step 7. To work the inward corners, clip the allowance right into the point of the corner. Sometimes students are afraid to do this for fear of having raw threads showing. It will not turn properly without being cut to the point. Fold under one edge to the point and stitch it.

Inward Corner

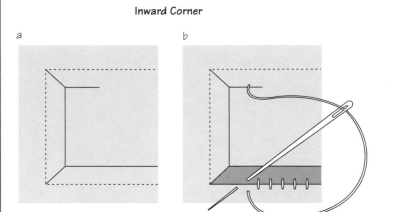

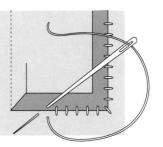

Take a diagonal stitch at the corner, turn the work, then fold and stitch the adjacent edge.

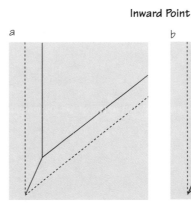

Inward Point

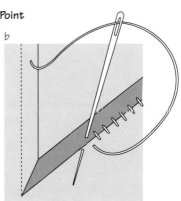

Use the same techniques at inward points.

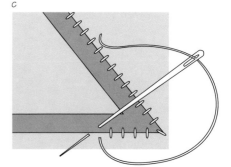

Step 8. Concave curves must be clipped before stitching. Smaller curves or circles need to have the clips closer together than larger curves.

Clipping Concave Curves and Circles

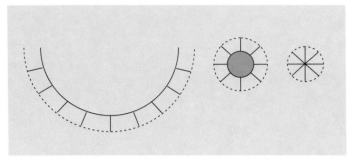

After clipping a curve, try holding the left side down with your left forefinger, and with your needle, fold the edge under in one swoop.

Folding Edge Under With Needle

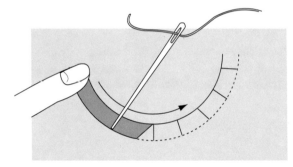

Step 9. Do not clip convex curves. If you do, undesired points can occur. Fold the edge under at the curve. Make one stitch and fold again. Make another stitch and fold.

Convex Curves

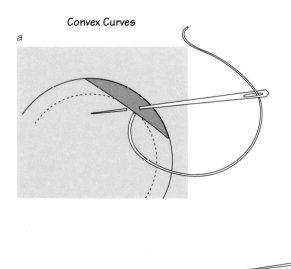

Continue this way along the curve—fold, stitch, fold, stitch. Remember to use the tip of the needle to grasp the folded edge as well as your fingers to refine the shape if needed, pushing it in or out to make a smooth curve.

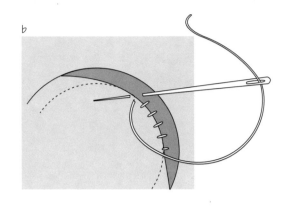

Step 10. To end your thread, make a loop on the top of the work and bring your thread through it. Insert needle at loop and bring it up through the fabric away from the knot. Cut the thread off with your scissors.

Ending Stitching

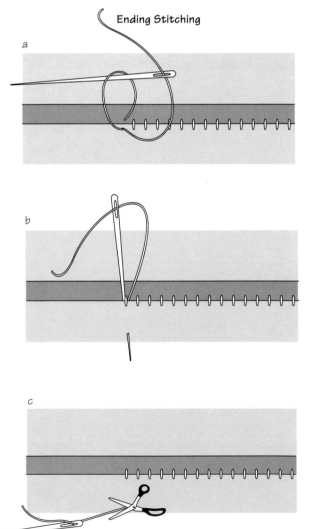

CHAPTER THREE

The Schoolhouse With Reverse Appliqué in One Color

Many people have heard unfavorable things about reverse appliqué from authors and speakers who seldom do it. Thus, the myth of difficulty is given validation. It is often described as being done with many layers. If only one color of appliqué is planned, one layer for the appliqué and one piece underneath will be needed. It need be no more difficult than any other appliqué.

The process of reverse appliqué occurs as follows: An opening is cut in one full layer over another layer or smaller piece of fabric and stitched, so that the image is revealed as the underneath fabric. The top layer then becomes the background surrounding the image. The stitching is done by cutting a little at a time. Cut, clip, fold, and stitch. The turn-under allowance is cut along the inside edge instead of the outside as in direct appliqué.

The Schoolhouse pattern offers a chance to find out how easy this is. In this book you will find more quilts done with reverse (negative) appliqué than with direct (positive) appliqué. I always feel that reverse appliqué is easier, because when you trace a design, no matter how complicated it may be, you do not have to worry about positioning the pieces accurately. Tracing and positioning are done in one step. Try one block and see.

The size given for the block is a bit larger than the final size. Besides the allowance of ¼" all around for seaming, I recommend adding another ¼" all around since appliqué has a tendency to shrink as you work. The image also tends to change size so that the result seldom matches the original pattern size exactly. Final trimming is done after the stitching is completed.

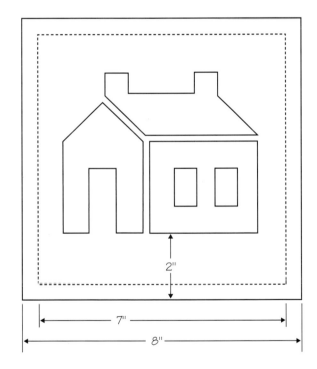

SCHOOLHOUSE OF ONE COLOR IN REVERSE APPLIQUÉ

Use Schoolhouse Pattern A
   Finished Size: 7" x 7"
   Materials: Two 8" x 8" squares of contrasting fabrics; thread to match top layer

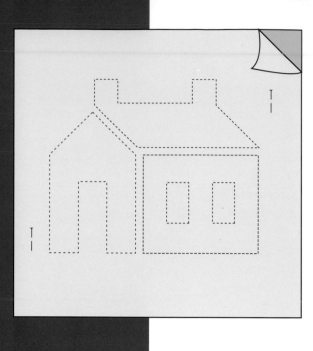

Step 1

Trace Schoolhouse Pattern A onto the top square, centering the schoolhouse and positioning the base of it 2" up from the bottom edge of the fabric as shown on the diagram of Pattern A on page 15. Pin this traced square to the square underneath, which will be the color of the schoolhouse.

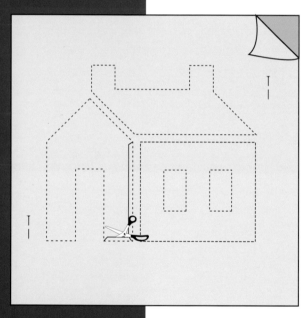

Step 2

Start cutting a turn-under allowance of ⅛" inside the front edge of the schoolhouse. Clip into the corners.

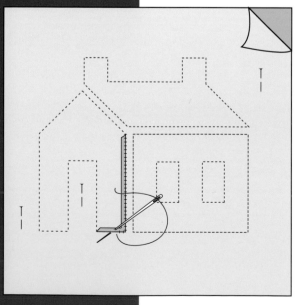

Step 3

Fold and stitch the edge under on the traced line. Refer to the stitch instructions in Chapter Two (page 10).

Step 4

Continue cutting, clipping, folding, and stitching. Turn the work as you stitch so you are in a comfortable position.

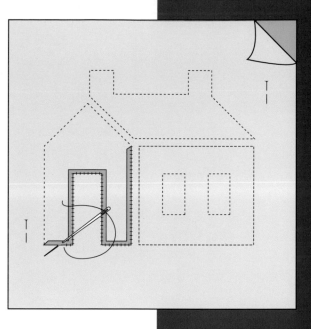

Step 5

Continue working until you are back to the starting point. Discard the cut-away piece.

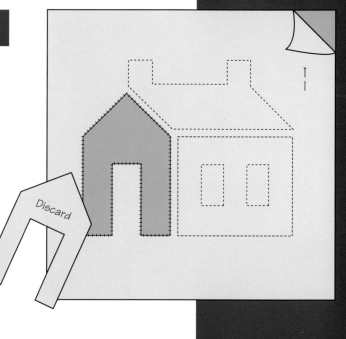

Step 6

Move your needle to the adjacent corner of the roof. Cut ⅛" inside of the roof, clip when necessary, fold under, and begin stitching the edge.

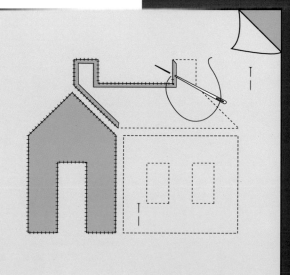

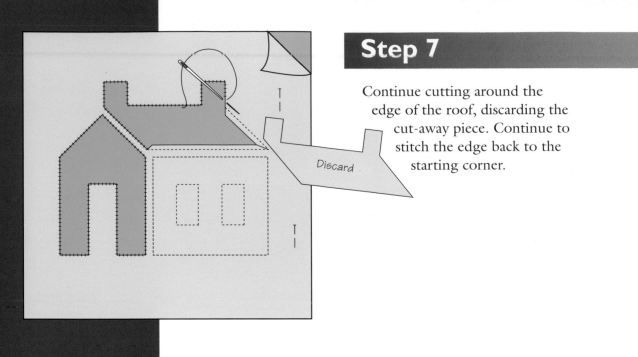

Step 7

Continue cutting around the edge of the roof, discarding the cut-away piece. Continue to stitch the edge back to the starting corner.

Discard

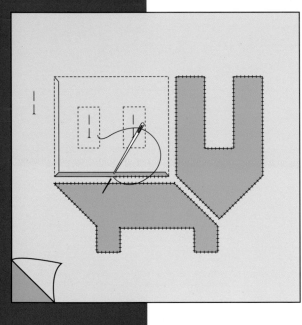

Step 8

Pin the two windows securely in place. Move the needle to the corner of the schoolhouse side nearest the place that you ended appliquéing the roof. Start cutting the turn-under allowance, folding and stitching it under. Always turn the piece as you work so that it is in a comfortable stitching position for you.

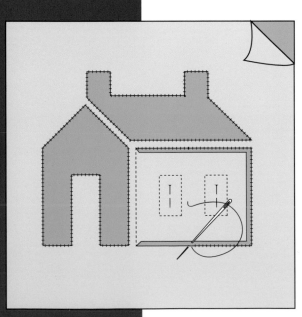

Step 9

Continue stitching around the edge of the side of the schoolhouse.

Step 10

The windows are already pinned in place. Cut around them with the same turn-under allowance and discard the cut-away piece.

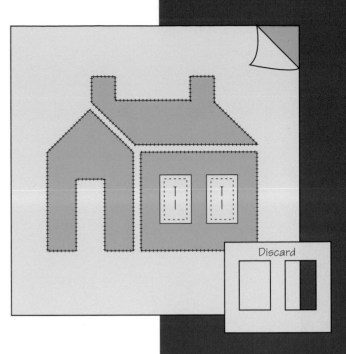

Step 11

Stitch down one window at a time. Here you will be "appliquéing" the windows to the schoolhouse.

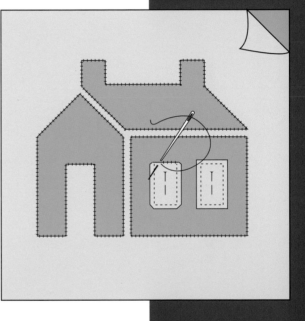

Step 12

Repeat with the second window.

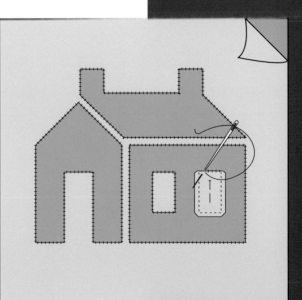

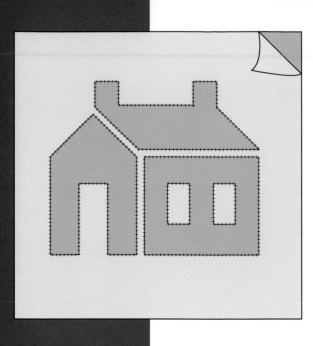

Step 13

The appliqué is now complete.

If you intend to use the block as an insert in a garment, pillow, or tote bag, you need not trim away the excess fabric. Cut the underneath fabric the same size as the top layer creating a self lining, which will add extra body to your project.

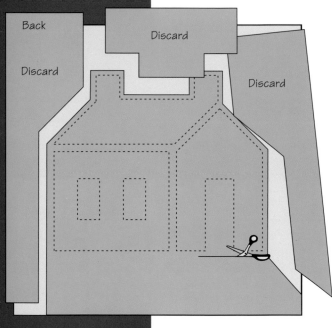

Step 14

If you are using the block for a quilt, you will probably want to cut away the excess fabric from the back to keep it light in weight. Turn the block over and carefully cut around the schoolhouse. Discard the waste fabric pieces.

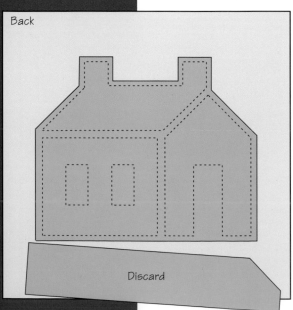

Step 15

Continue cutting away the excess fabric. To avoid excessive waste I usually cut my underneath fabric piece smaller than the top layer. Press the block and trim it with a rotary cutter to measure $7\frac{1}{2}$" x $7\frac{1}{2}$". Mark a $\frac{1}{4}$" seam allowance if desired.

Nostalgia. 1991. 26" x 30". Hand quilted.

For this quilt, I chose plaids. They reminded me
of the plaid skirts I often wore to school and of the
plaid uniforms schoolgirls sometimes wear.

Don't Sit Under the Apple Tree. 1986. 47" x 47".
Hand quilted. Collection of Jeanne and Gordon Rosenberry.

STRIP-PIECED VARIATION

The first Schoolhouse quilt that I made was *Don't Sit Under the Apple Tree.*

As an experiment I designed my first School-house pattern to accommodate a strip-pieced underlayer. The strips measure just under 1" when seamed. I designed the pattern to fit eight strips. After making several blocks, I had to decide how to use them. At the time I was naming most of my

Don't Sit Under the Apple Tree. Two Blocks

quilts after Glenn Miller's top hit songs. I could not think of an appropriate song title until I realized that I was using colors, similar to the Apple™ Computer logo. That gave me the idea of designing an apple tree to go with my blocks as a central medallion. Hence, the song title, popular during World War II. The song lyrics demanded that a seat be placed under the tree to be reserved by a soldier's sweetheart until his return from the war. I added a swing for this purpose.

In making more School-house blocks for the quilt, I decided to vary the blocks to avoid monotony, which is why I reversed the sequence of the strip colors on half of them. For more variety, I did the corner blocks as appliqué. In other words, I made four strip-pieced squares large enough for the four corner blocks and then appliquéd four black school-houses to them as described in Chapter Five.

STRIP-PIECED HOUSE

Use Schoolhouse Pattern B

Finished Size: 9½" x 9½"

Materials: One 10½" x 10½" square of fabric (top layer); six strips 9" x 1½", two strips 9" x 2" (the first and last strips include extra seam allowance.) These strips may be all different colors, four each of two colors or two each of four colors; thread to match the square.

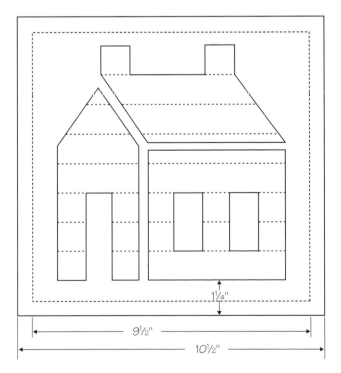

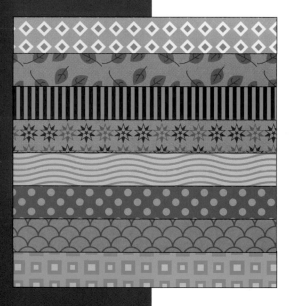

Step 1

Lay out the strips in the desired order for seaming. The two wider strips should be at the top and bottom.

Step 2

Seam the strips together on the sewing machine with ¼" seam allowances. Press the resulting square in one direction. Measure the widths of the strips with the dotted lines of the pattern to make sure they are straight and accurate. If not, rip them out and re-sew any irregular ones to match the pattern lines.

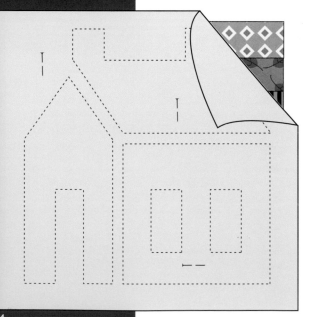

Step 3

Trace Schoolhouse Pattern B onto the top-layer fabric square, centering it, and placing the bottom of the schoolhouse 1¼" from the bottom edge of the fabric. Do not trace the dotted lines inside the schoolhouse. Pin this traced fabric square to the strip-pieced underlayer. Hold it up to a light or lay it on a light box to make sure that the seams are straight and that the chimneys, door, and windows line up with the seams of the underlayer, as shown by the dotted lines of the pattern. This will avoid awkward spaces from occurring at these points.

Step 4

Starting with the front of the schoolhouse, cut the inside turn-under allowance and stitch it under as in Steps 2, 3, 4, and 5 of the previous directions (pages 16–17).

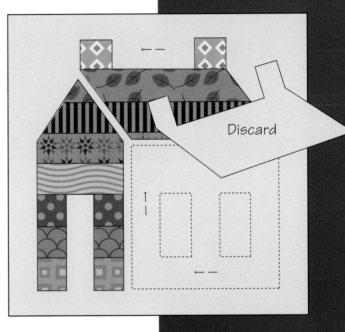

Step 5

Repeat with the roof of the schoolhouse as directed in Steps 6 and 7 in the previous directions on pages 17–18. Make sure the edges of the roof correspond to the seams of the underlayer as indicated on the pattern.

Step 6

Continue with the side of the school-house and the windows, following Steps 8, 9, 10, 11 and 12 of the previous directions (pages 18–19). If all goes well, your chimneys, windows, and door will be lined up as shown on the pattern. If you are a little off here or there, it probably will not matter—it adds a little character! Press the block and trim it with a rotary cutter to measure 10" x 10." Mark a ¼" seam allowance if desired.

Rainbow Houses. 1987. 37" x 48". Hand quilted.

STRING-PIECED VARIATION

After using the strip-pieced method to make the underlayer with even strips, I decided to forget the precision and use some of my various-sized scrap strips or "strings" without worrying about lining them up accurately. I dove into my scrap pile and pieced them at random, using the uneven strips as they were, sometimes piecing shorter pieces to form longer strips. I kept working quickly, without concern about how colors went together. I find this provides a needed catharsis on those sluggish days when I don't feel like working. It's fun! When I had a few squares, I stitched them up with schoolhouses. I realized that it gave them a dilapidated look. They reminded me of a visit to the ghost town of Bodie, California. I decided to make a quilt, and I named it *Ghost Town*.

Several years later, an earthquake hit several places in the San Francisco Bay Area. I had moved safely to the Sierra foothills. At the time the quake hit, I was piecing several of these blocks to make as examples for workshops. I went on to make more "decrepit" Schoolhouse blocks. I also decided to make more squares of random strip-piecing without schoolhouses just because it was fun, and it is always a good feeling to use all the accumulated scraps. When I began to lay these out with the Schoolhouse blocks, it hit me that they were beginning to resemble an earthquake. I then continued to make more, and they became an earthquake quilt

I made another quilt called *Rainbow Houses* using the same method. This time I repeated the same block with no variations. If you wish to make multiple blocks for a quilt, cut your strips from the entire width of the fabric—from selvage to selvage. Fold the fabric and be sure the cut edge is squared up with the fold and selvages. Check this with your cutting ruler. Cut your strips as needed, 1½" or 2" across. Seam the strips, press them, and then with a ruler, cut them into 9" sections. You will be able to get four squares from the fabric width.

Ghost Town, Two Blocks.

Ghost Town, 1987. 43" x 43".
Hand quilted. Collection of Dena Canty .

with several house parts flying around. The strange thing is that as I worked on the quilt shown on page 28, it kept getting askew unintentionally. I meant to have even borders but somehow they were not. The corner squares became different sizes. Instead of making them even with ripping and re-sewing, I decided to leave them crooked and to go along with the uncontrolled feeling of chaos. Without realizing it, I even signed my name to the wrong corner. I decided that this was meant to be. Maybe you would like to make a few derelict Schoolhouse blocks for your own ghost town or disaster quilt.

Earthquake. 1990. 52" x 52". Hand quilted .

STRING-PIECED SCHOOLHOUSE

Use Schoolhouse Pattern B
Finished Size: 9½" x 9½"
Materials: One 10½" x 10½" square;
multi-colored scrap strips; thread to match the square

Step 1

Dig into your scraps and bring out any strips you have or cut some strips from your large scraps. Seam them together randomly to form a 9" square. Sometimes you may want to stitch some pieces together before you cut them into strips or piece together short strips to form long ones. Press them flat.

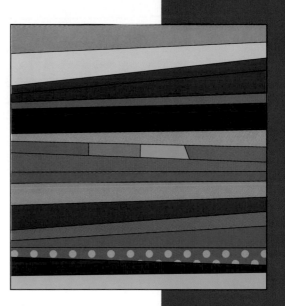

Step 2

Trace Schoolhouse Pattern B onto the top-layer square, centering it, and placing the bottom edge of the schoolhouse 1¼" from the bottom edge of the fabric. Do not trace the dotted lines inside the schoolhouse. Pin this traced square over the pieced square making sure that it is centered under the schoolhouse with enough allowance all around for pinning.

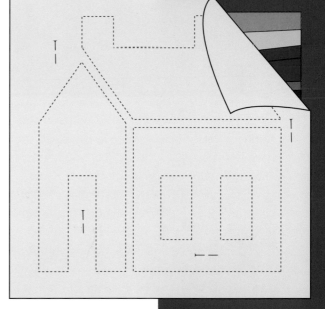

Step 3

Repeat the same procedure as given in the directions on pages 16–19.

CHAPTER FOUR

The Schoolhouse With Reverse Appliqué in Three Colors

When reverse appliqué is done with several colors, most people believe that layers of all the colors are first basted together. Reverse appliqué is often likened to the molas made by the Kuna Indians of Panama. Mola making is often mistakenly explained that way by well-meaning people who repeat only what they have heard. When I first started experimenting with reverse appliqué, before I began examining the mola methods used by the Kuna Indians, I tried basting the layers first and found it extremely awkward. After about six attempts, I abandoned that method and began to place the pieces beneath the top layer only where I wanted them to be exposed. There is no reason to waste a whole layer of fabric with most of it serving no purpose.

Adding smaller pieces underneath one at a time as I work makes a lot more sense. The Kunas always use one layer underneath to give the whole piece body since the molas are sewn into their blouses. It serves as a lining. One or two other layers are built up in between the top and the foundation layer when they are exposed throughout the whole design surface. Additional colors are added with small inserts under the top layer, and they have plenty of outlined double appliqué details on the top layer. Sometimes the direct appliqué is featured more than reverse appliqué, but this characteristic is often ignored as reverse appliqué is emphasized, creating more awe and wonder. The designs in this book do not contain the complexity of the molas. Reverse appliqué can be very simple as presented in the quilts in this book. It is not the same as mola work.

Make one of these schoolhouses with reverse appliqué of several colors and see if you agree. Like me, you may decide it is often easier than regular appliqué because the three parts are drawn in position on one piece and they can not get out of position.

SCHOOLHOUSE OF THREE COLORS IN REVERSE APPLIQUÉ

Use Schoolhouse Pattern A

Finished Block Size: 7" x 7"

Materials: One 8" x 8" square of fabric (top layer); three smaller pieces, each sized to cover each part of the schoolhouse (the diagrams show a rectangle but any shaped scrap can be used if it is large enough); thread to match the square.

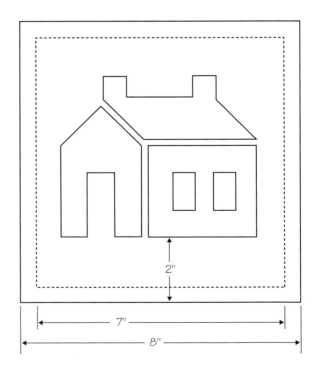

Step 1

An 8" square allows for seaming and any shrinking that may occur as you work. This will be the top layer or background around the schoolhouse. Trace Schoolhouse Pattern A onto the square, centering it, and positioning the base of the house 2" from the bottom edge of the fabric. Cut a piece of fabric that is large enough to cover the schoolhouse front with ample space around it for pinning. Position it behind the traced schoolhouse front.

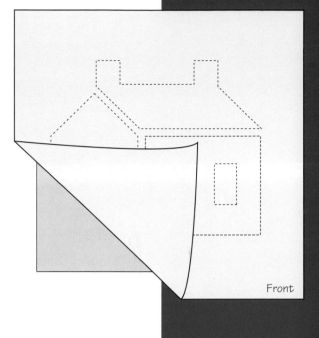

Front

Step 2

Pin the scrap on the back. Turn it over and hold the piece up to the light to make sure it covers well.

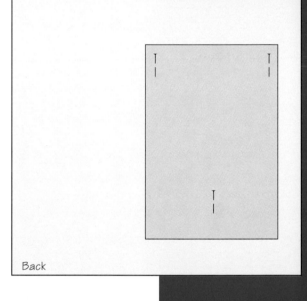

Back

Step 3

Start cutting ⅛" from the inside edge of the schoolhouse front. If you start at the corner where the three schoolhouse parts meet you can continue reverse appliquéing without breaking your thread to begin the next part.

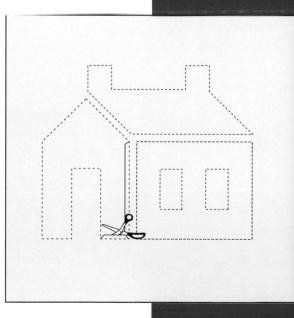

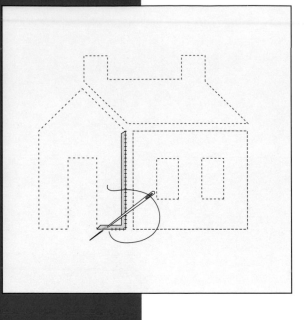

Step 4

Fold the edge under on the traced line and begin stitching with small, even stitches.

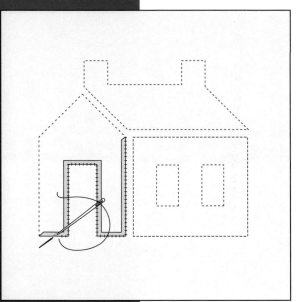

Step 5

Continue cutting, folding and stitching around the doorway, clipping and trimming as needed.

Discard

Step 6

Continue this way back to the starting point, and discard the cut-away fabric from the top surface.

Step 7

Turn the piece over to the back.

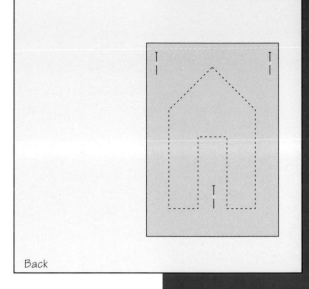

Step 8

Trim away the excess fabric around the schoolhouse front, leaving about ⅛" around it. Discard the excess fabric pieces.

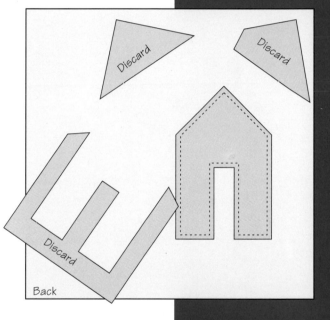

Step 9

Repeat this same procedure with the roof of the schoolhouse. Cut a piece large enough, position it on the back being sure it covers the whole roof area, and pin it in place on the back.

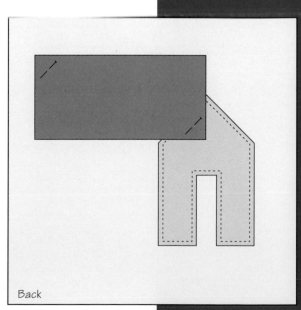

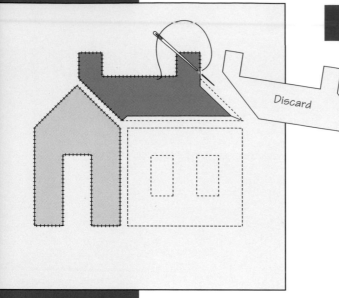

Step 10

Turn the work to the front. Cut, fold, and stitch the roof edge under, discarding the cut-away piece.

Discard

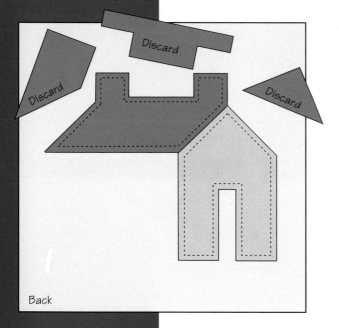

Discard

Discard

Discard

Back

Step 11

When the roof is stitched, turn it over to the back, trim away, and discard the excess fabric pieces.

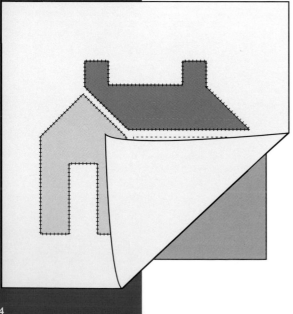

Step 12

Cut a third piece large enough for the side of the schoolhouse, and position it behind that side.

Step 13

Pin the scrap in place on the back. Check to make sure it covers with enough allowance for pinning.

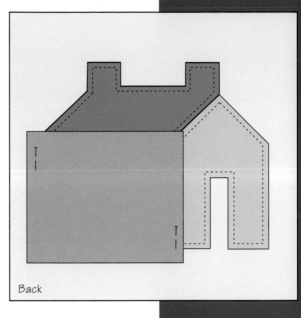

Back

Step 14

Turn the work over to the front and pin the two windows in place to the underneath piece. Start cutting, folding, and stitching the inside edge around the school-house side.

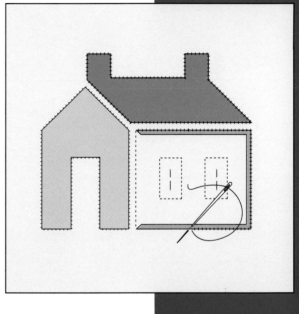

Step 15

Cut around the two windows with the same turn-under allowance while keeping them pinned in place. Discard the cut-away piece.

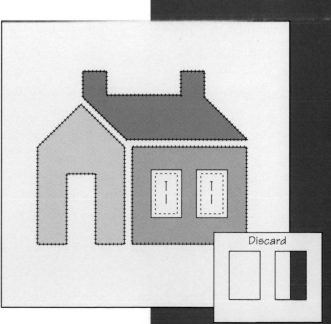

Discard

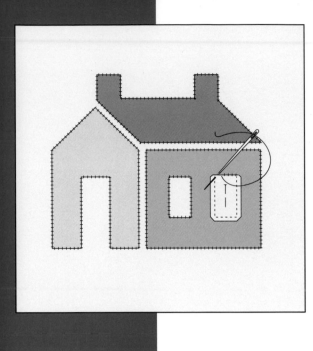

Step 16

Trim the corners of the window. Stitch the turn-under allowance under around each window, appliquéing them to the exposed side of the schoolhouse.

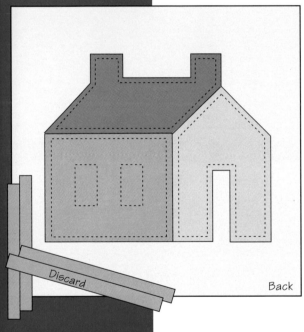

Discard

Back

Step 17

Turn the work over to the back, and trim away the excess fabric about ⅛" around the edge. Discard the excess fabric pieces.

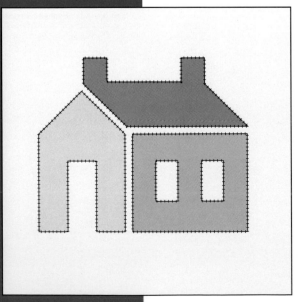

Step 18

Press the block and trim it with a rotary cutter to measure 7½" x 7½".

The Neighborhood. 1988. 42" x 42". Hand quilted.

This quilt, *The Neighborhood*, was made with blocks of three-color schoolhouses combined with the traditional quilt pattern, Attic Windows. The window uprights were made of hand-dyed gradated fabrics. Many hand dyers offer their products to quilters, and it provides one more dimension to the achievement of special effects.

My Kind of Town. 1988. 46" x 46". Hand quilted.

I combined the three-color schoolhouse with the strip-pieced schoolhouse in Chapter 3 and made the quilt, *My Kind of Town*. I used soft tan for the top layer (background) around the schoolhouses but found I did not have enough for 12 blocks. Since I could no longer match it, I used a lighter shade of tan for four of them. I placed these lighter squares in the center of the quilt and was delighted that I had not had enough of the "right" color for the last four squares. I often find that when the desired fabric does not stretch far enough, it is a wonderful challenge to find another idea, which can often result in a better solution than the original one.

Katie's Kind of Town. 1989. 48" x 48". Hand quilted.

I admired Katie Pasquini-Masopust's hand-silk-screened fabrics. Until I bought some from her, I used only solids since the delicate floral prints available at that time did not fit into the strong graphic images that I preferred. When I learned that she was offering a class in silk-screening, I learned this useful process from her. I then turned my garage into a printing house. Finally, I was able to produce fabric that I liked—small geometric prints. All of this led to the making of *Katie's Kind of Town*. This quilt combines Katie's printed fabric, prints that I made in her class, and a few commercial prints. This was the beginning of my eventual lure away from solid-colored fabrics.

CHAPTER
FIVE

The Schoolhouse With Appliqué in One Color

When doing an appliqué with more than one part of the same color in close proximity, I like to trace the whole design (all the parts) to one piece of fabric as one unit instead of tracing them to separate pieces. This way, they are more apt to stay in the proper position. I cut the allowance as I work. When precutting, details can drift out of position and must be pinned or basted. You can stitch very complicated, intricate designs without basting or much pinning by delaying the final cutting of the turn-under allowances until you are ready to stitch them. By delaying the cutting, everything stays where you placed it. I prefer this cut-as-you-go for all types of appliqué.

SCHOOLHOUSE OF ONE COLOR IN APPLIQUÉ

Use Schoolhouse Pattern A

Finished Block Size: 7" x 7"

Materials: One 8" x 8" square of fabric (foundation or underneath layer); one 5" x 6" piece in a contrasting color (appliqué piece); thread to match the appliqué

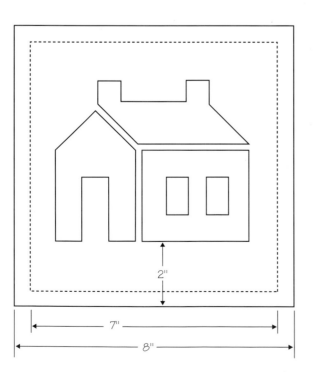

40

Step 1

Trace Schoolhouse Pattern A onto the piece of appliqué fabric. Pin the traced fabric to the foundation square centering it and positioning the bottom edge of the schoolhouse 2" from the bottom edge of the square. An extra inch is added to the foundation for seaming and for any shrinking that may occur while working.

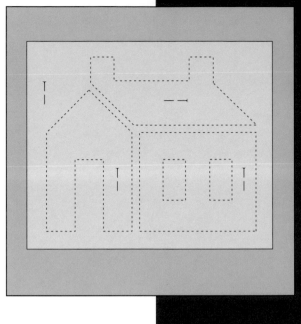

Step 2

Start cutting between two schoolhouse parts. This should give you an allowance of ⅛" to fold under.

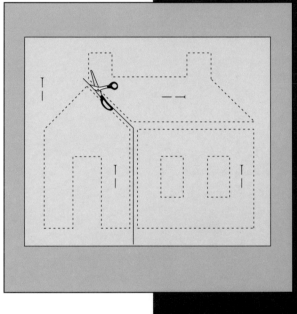

Step 3

Fold the edge under and start making fine, even stitches around the piece. I suggest starting at the point where the front, side, and roof meet. The diagram shows working the front first.

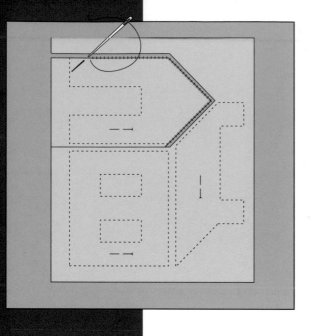

Step 4

Continue stitching around the piece. Turn the work as necessary for comfortable stitching.

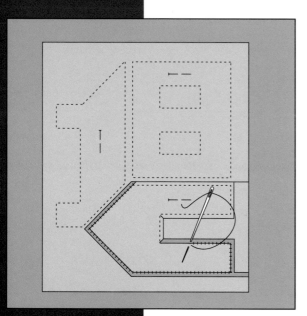

Step 5

Continue cutting, clipping the corners, folding, and stitching, forming the doorway.

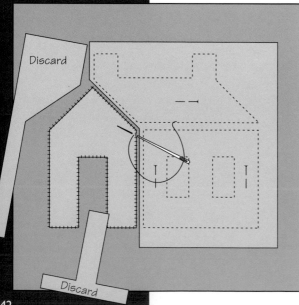

Discard

Discard

Step 6

Discard excess fabric pieces as you cut and stitch. Move the pins when necessary as you cut to hold loose parts in position. Continue back to your starting point.

Step 7

Cut between the two remaining parts.

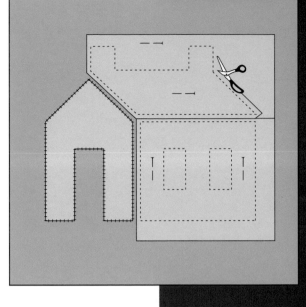

Step 8

Stitch around the second part as you did before, cutting away waste fabric. Turn the work when needed so you are not in an awkward position as you work.

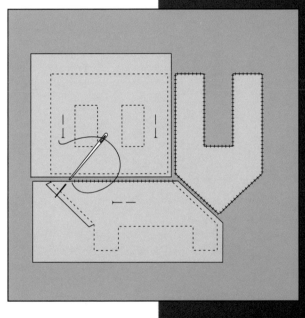

Step 9

Discard excess fabric pieces as you work back to the starting place.

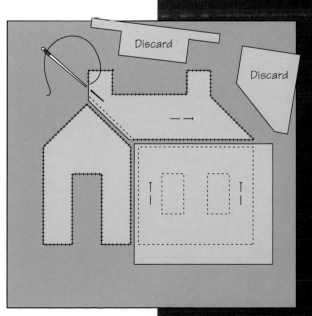

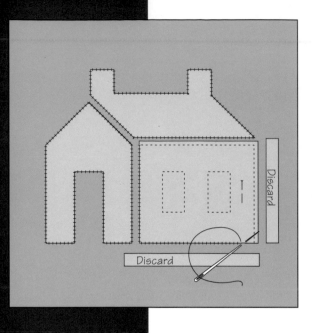

Step 10

Repeat Steps 8–9 with the third section of the schoolhouse.

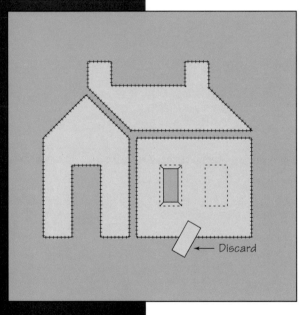

Step 11

Now you are ready to work the windows. Sometimes, there are cut-outs in an appliqué piece, and people often call this reverse appliqué. But these are what they are—cut-outs. With the tip of your scissors, lift the fabric within one window away from the foundation. Cut away the inside of the window, leaving a turn-under allowance of ⅛", and clip the corners.

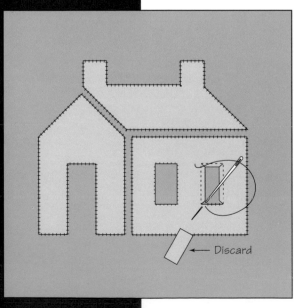

Step 12

Fold the edge under, stitch it, and repeat this for the second window.

Press the block and trim it with a rotary cutter to measure 7½" x 7½", allowing ¼" seam allowance on all sides.

My Greatest Fear. 1994. 19" x 19". Machine quilted.

I made this quilted wall hanging, *My Greatest Fear,* as a response to so many disasters occurring all over the country. One of my great fears is to be without my comfortable home, my cozy studio and my treasured fabric collection. When I hear of a devastating event, I think of the quilters who are losing their wonderful collection of quilting necessities. The place where I live is in a dangerous fire area. That is foremost in my mind during the dry summers. Earthquakes are uncommon. However, the very morning after completing this piece, a very long rumbling earthquake occurred close enough to generate new feelings of fear. I found several appropriate printed fabrics to express the four catastrophes we have been hearing about too frequently in the news.

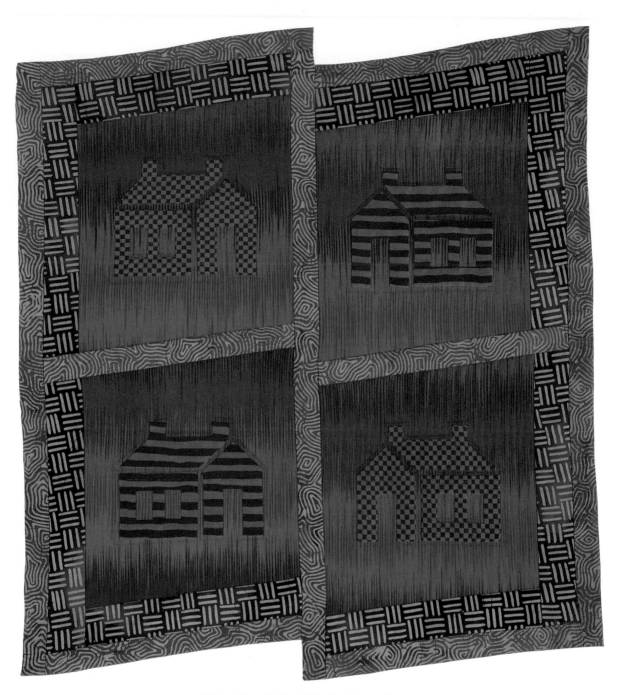

P.U.D. 1994. 22" x 25". Machine quilted.

I named this piece *P.U.D.* Anyone who lives in a townhouse and serves his or her dutiful stint on the association's board of directors, knows what that means: "Planned Unit Development." The houses are always similar, but cleverly painted or finished to look different, one from the other, without steady repeats. This piece was made to utilize one of my favorite fat quarters of fabric, cut into smaller quarters. It was made right after *My Greatest Fear* and may have had some residual earthquake anxiety worked into it.

Most often I like to make the Schoolhouse pattern with three colors, one for each part, the front, side, and roof. The appliqué schoolhouse made of three colors is worked in a way similar to that with one color, except that each piece is traced to a different color of fabric. This is a good way to use up some of your favorite scraps. They must be large enough so the turn-under allowance can be cut around each piece. As with the schoolhouse of one color in Chapter Five, I like to cut the final turn-under allowance as I work.

SCHOOLHOUSE OF THREE COLORS IN APPLIQUÉ

Use Schoolhouse Pattern A

Finished Block Size: 7" x 7"

Materials: One 8" x 8" square of fabric (foundation or underneath layer); three pieces in contrasting colors, large enough for each part of the schoolhouse (appliqué parts); thread to match the three appliqué pieces

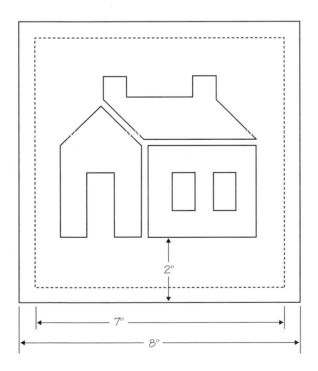

The 8" square of foundation fabric allows for seaming and for any shrinking that may occur while working.

The diagrams show rectangular-shaped pieces but any shaped scrap will do.

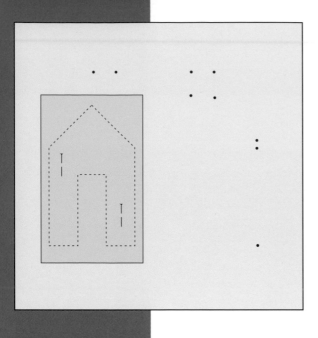

Step 1

Position Schoolhouse Pattern A over the foundation square, centering it and placing the bottom edge of the schoolhouse 2" up from the bottom edge of the fabric. Trace very tiny dots, scarcely visible to indicate the position of the corners of the schoolhouse onto this fabric. Trace the front of the schoolhouse onto a piece large enough to have a turn-under allowance around it of at least ⅛". Pin the traced front piece in position on the block.

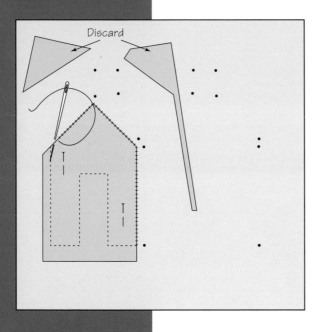

Discard

Step 2

Start cutting around the piece with a turn-under allowance of ⅛". Fold under the allowance and start stitching. Cut away and discard the excess fabric as you stitch.

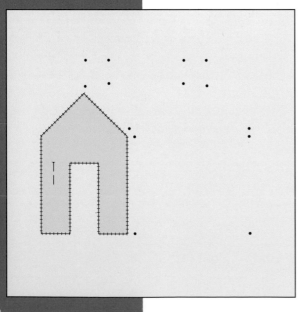

Step 3

Continue around the front to the starting point.

Step 4

Trace the roof onto another color of scrap, making sure it is large enough for a turn-under allowance of ⅛" all around. Pin it in position matching the corners to the marks as closely as possible.

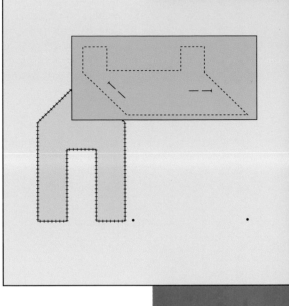

Step 5

Change the thread color to match the roof fabric. Start cutting and stitching a little at a time. Discard the excess fabric as you stitch.

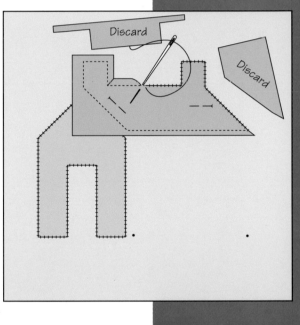

Step 6

Continue cutting and stitching back to the starting point.

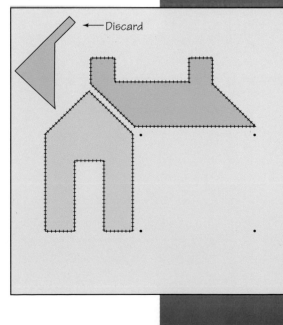

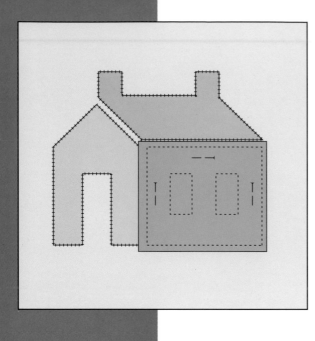

Step 7

Trace the side of the school-house onto a third color of fabric. Pin it in position on the block.

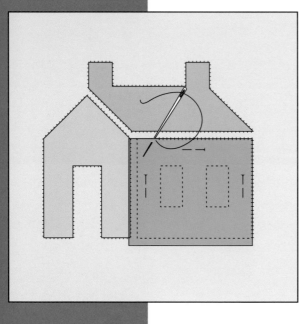

Step 8

Fold and stitch the turn-under allowance, trimming as needed around the edge.

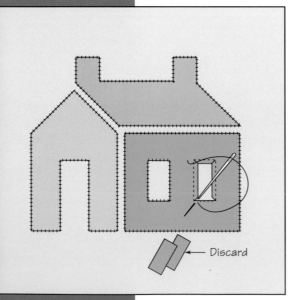

Discard

Step 9

After the side of the school-house is completed, cut away the insides of the windows one at a time and stitch them under as in Steps 11 and 12 in Chapter Five (page 44). Press the block and trim it with a rotary cutter to measure $7\frac{1}{2}$" x $7\frac{1}{2}$".

Fantasyland. 1994. 31" x 41". Machine quilted.

Fantasyland was made as my own personal celebration of many enjoyable trips to my favorite fabric shops. The fabrics today inspire so many ideas. Before I can use the fat quarters that I have accumulated, more tempting prints come on the market. This quilt was an attempt to create a whole fabric neighborhood that lurks in my imagination where I walk around a world made of my favorite fabrics.

Hillside. 1994. 32" x 38". Hand quilted.

Hillside. Two Blocks. The blue schoolhouse is reverse
appliqué while the orange one is appliqué.

While making the quilts for this book, I used reverse appliqué for most of them. The quilt *Hillside* combines appliqué schoolhouses on half of the blocks with reverse appliqué schoolhouses for the other half.

I thought it would be interesting to work with both methods on one quilt as a contrast. I staggered the blocks to get away from the usual quilt format, and it gave me the impression of houses on a hill. Try different arrangements to see what you can discover. You can change the lighting on the house by switching the light and dark fabrics. With *Hillside,* I used a rainbow range of fabrics in the three different tones arranged on dark backgrounds so the light source always would seem to come from the same position.

Enhancements

Now that you have tried making schoolhouses by different methods, you may wish to try something less rigid. Combine these blocks with the letters of the alphabet, as I have, or perhaps a tree can be combined with the schoolhouse for a special project you would like to make. Patterns are given for the letters and the tree. They are worked in a similar way. The Tree pattern and some of the letters will give you practice with curves and circles. Refer to the stitch diagrams in Chapter Two (page 14) for hints on how to handle them.

As I walk around my neighborhood, I am grateful for the magnificent trees. Nothing makes a street of houses more pleasant. Try working the Tree pattern as appliqué and reverse appliqué. Trace it onto a piece of fabric, position it over a 10½" square, and pin. Refer to Chapter Five (page 40) for appliquéing.

Tree House. Two Blocks.

If you want to try it as reverse appliqué, cut a top layer 10½" x 10½" and center the Tree pattern. Trace it. Refer to Chapter Three (page 15) for reverse appliquéing.

Tree House. 1988. 40" x 40". Hand quilted.

For this quilt, *Tree House,* I wanted to try more variations of the strip-pieced schoolhouse. I also wanted to try strip-pieced trees. You may find many other ways of positioning the Tree pattern with schoolhouses. I used rigid rows but you may want to add many trees around one schoolhouse and create a more informal design. Make some trees of reverse appliqué and then appliqué additional trees over them to create more depth.

Letters, Appliqué Block. Marbelized Fabrics
by Sonya Lee Barrington.

The letters of the alphabet are given so that
you can add names, initials, or special words to a
piece of appliqué work. The letters at the left are
the initials of my town and county. You may think
of many reasons to add letters for banners or
quilts for special events. You can use the letters
for many other quilts—to spell out the name of a
child or the family if you are ambitious or to spell
a special occasion such as "Happy Birthday!"

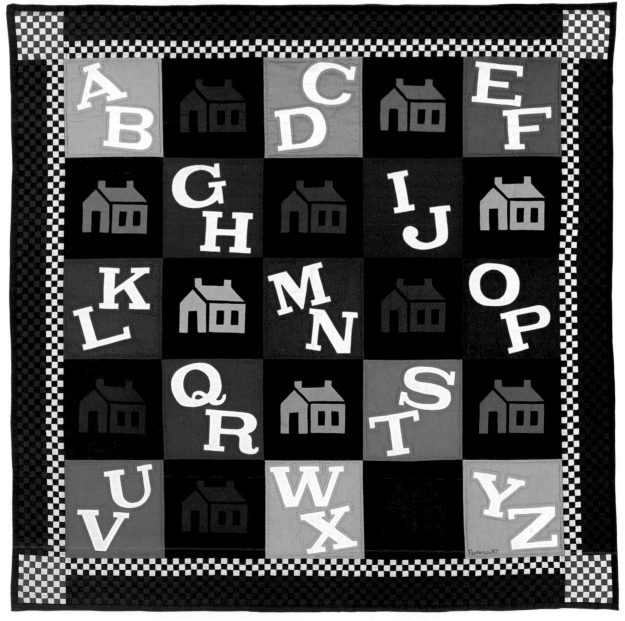

School Days. 1987. 49" x 49". Hand quilted.

ABC's. 1991. 28" x 33". Hand quilted.

Schoolhouses and the ABC's just go together. Both of these quilts would be nice for a small pre-school child first learning the alphabet. It is nice to be able to combine lettering with the school-houses or with any other kind of design. I find that the letters are more successful as direct appliqué than reverse appliqué. They require a bit more accuracy. You may want to try them in reverse appliqué as well.

ONE LETTER BLOCK

Use any Letter Pattern
 Suggested Finished Block Size: 7" x 7"
 Materials: One 8" x 8" square (foundation); any contrasting piece large enough to accommodate the letter you choose in a contrasting color; thread to match the appliqué piece

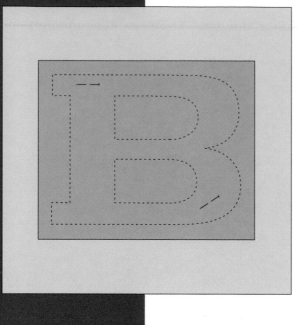

Step 1

Trace the letter onto a piece of fabric sized a bit larger than the letter. Pin this to the foundation fabric square.

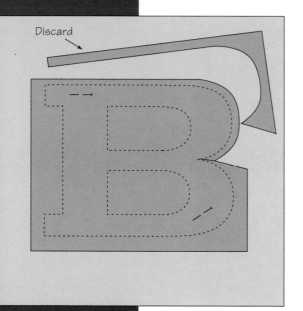

Discard

Step 2

Start cutting around the letter, leaving a turn-under allowance of ⅛". Discard the excess cut-away fabric pieces.

Step 3

Fold under the allowance on the traced line and stitch.

Step 4

Continue back to your starting place, cutting, folding, stitching, and discarding excess cut-away fabric pieces as you work.

Step 5

Cut and stitch any cut-outs in the letters as you did with the windows in the Schoolhouse patterns (page 44). Press the block and trim it with a rotary cutter to measure 7½" x 7½".

Discard

Step 6

You are now ready to combine letters with schoolhouses to make a quilt for whatever purpose.

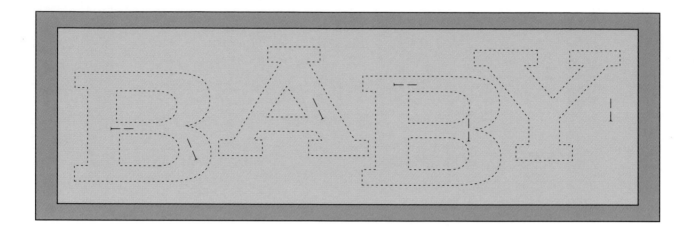

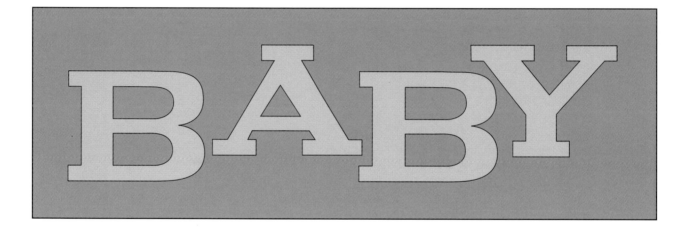

Also, you may want to use several letters to spell out a word as one unit.

Choose the letters you need and make a tracing of them on one sheet of paper to spell out the desired word. You can make them in a straight line. I think it is easier to let the letters bounce a little so that you do not have to be so concerned with perfect letter spacing, which demands a practiced eye to make the word read properly. It is also a bit more difficult to keep the word in a perfectly straight line while appliquéing it. Trace the letters together on one piece of fabric. Then pin this to your foundation fabric. Start stitching, cutting each

letter with the turn-under allowance a little at a time as you work. Reposition pins as required.

Try using short simple words or initials on your quilt. Remember to change sizes when needed with a copy machine as described on page 9.

Sometimes a word may be too long to fit your space. If you reduce the letters, you will find a size that works. However, remember that if you make them too small, they may be too intricate to appliqué. It may take some trial and error of sizing and arrangement before you can get the words to the size you need.

Sun Valley School Quilt. 1989. 50" x 60". Stenciled and made by
the fifth grade, their parents and teachers. Designed and directed
by Susan Bradford. Collection of Bara Joses.

Susan Bradford had a different idea. When
the fifth grade of Sun Valley School in San Rafael,
California, needed money for an environmental
field trip, Susan organized this quilt for a coopera-
tive effort, to be raffled. She decided to have the
schoolhouses and alphabet as well as hearts stenciled by the children, their teachers, and parents.
Susan designed the quilt to fit the talents of the
workers. Those who could sew made the Nine
Patches for the corners and the half-square
triangle blocks; the children stenciled the letters;
the teachers stenciled the schoolhouses and hearts.
Most of the quilt was tied but some of the letters
are quilted, and Susan machine quilted the borders
and bound its edges. Raffling the quilt brought in
$500. The winner returned the quilt to the young
girl who sold her the ticket. Susan designed a special
back so that everyone who worked on the quilt
could sign it. It was a lesson in quiltmaking as well
as a money maker.

Quilting ¼" From Outside Edge of Appliqué

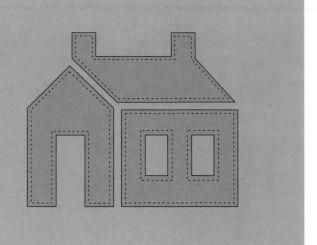

Quilting ¼" From Inside Edge of Reverse Appliqué

QUILTING THE APPLIQUÉ

When quilting by hand or machine, I always quilt around the thinner edge of the house. In other words, I usually quilt ¼" from the outside edge of the appliqué schoolhouse or tree. When quilting reverse appliqué, I usually quilt ¼" from the inside edge. Occasionally, I quilt in-the-ditch (right in the seam line on the side that has the least layers of fabric).

The Schoolhouse combines very well with many favorite traditional quilt patterns. Some suggestions are on the facing page. Look through quilt patterns and see if you can find a good way of combining the Schoolhouse block with some of your special favorites.

I hope that you will enjoy new ways of making Schoolhouse quilts and working these blocks into gifts for children, housewarming gifts, clothing and home accessories. May you find it as rewarding as I have, and always let it symbolize the comfortable old adage:

**"THERE'S NO PLACE
LIKE HOME!"**

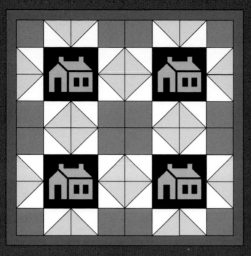

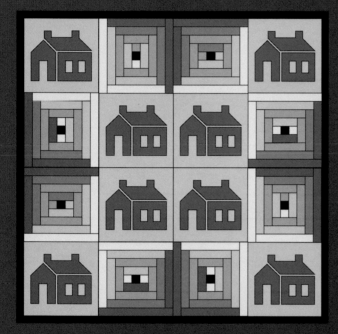

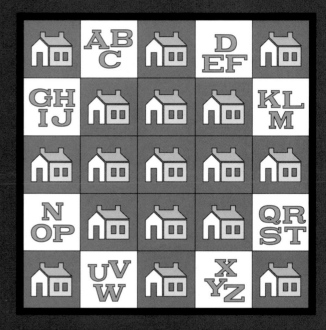

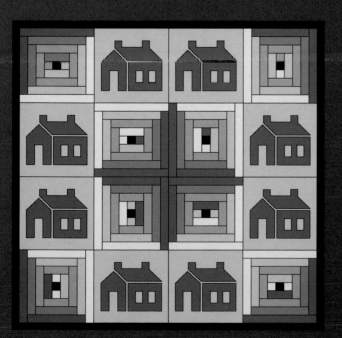

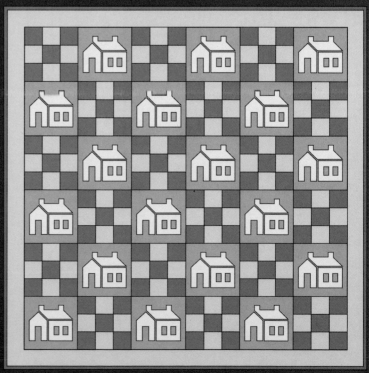

PATTERN A

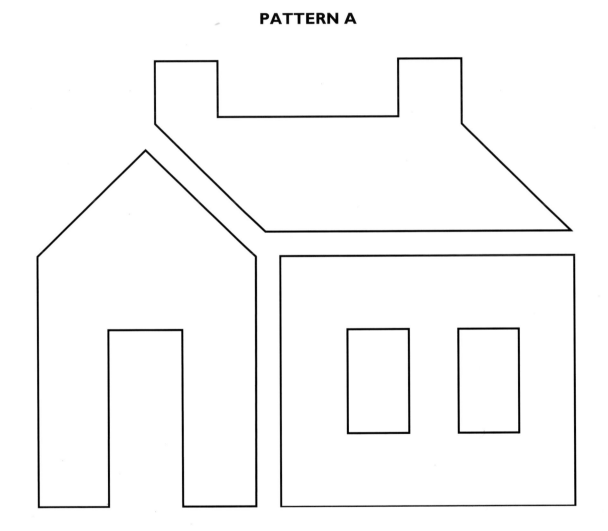

PATTERN B

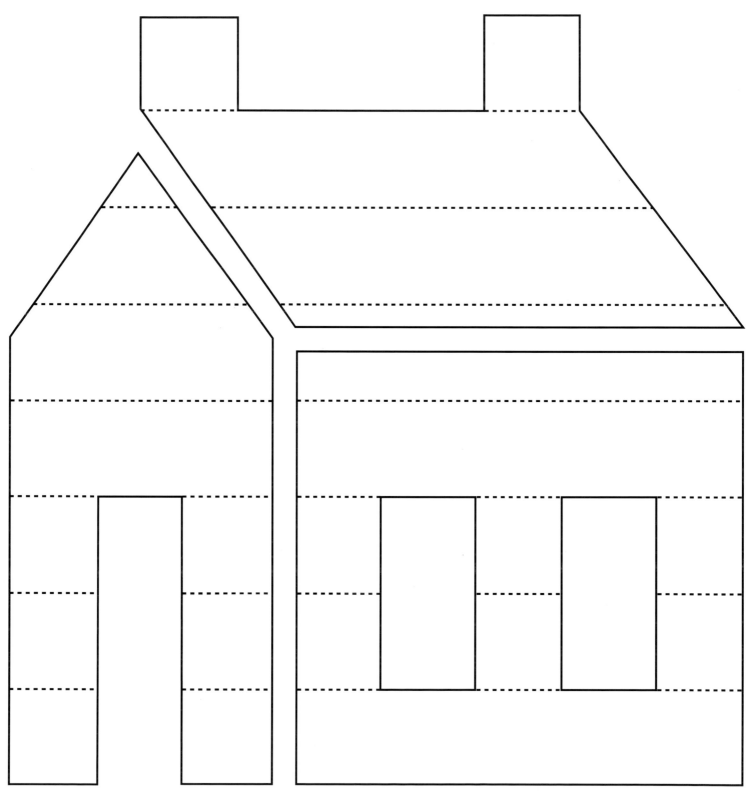

The Patterns

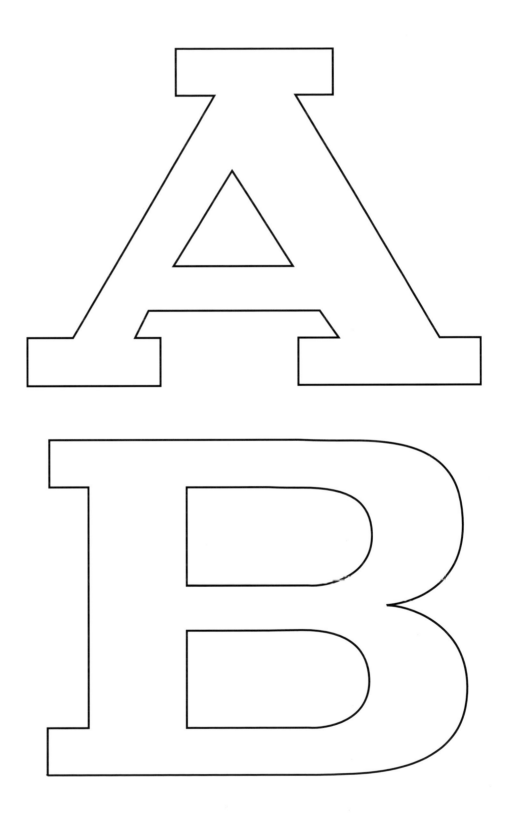

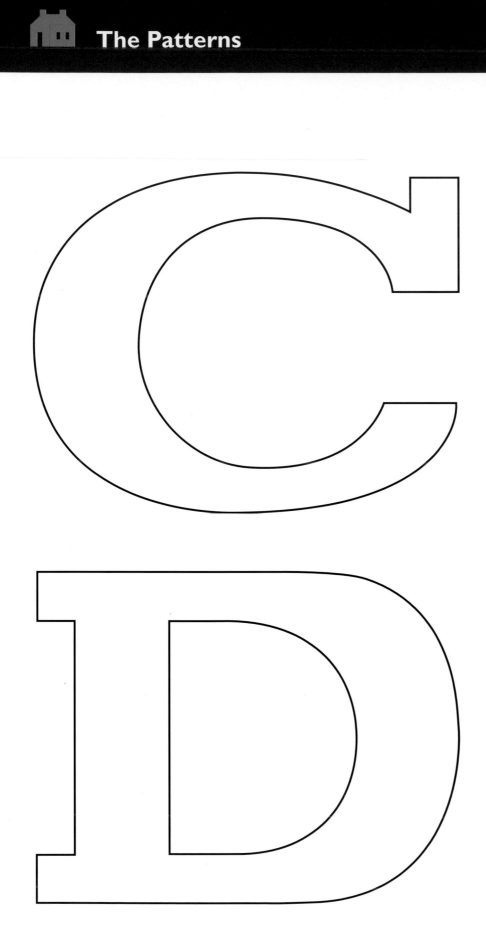

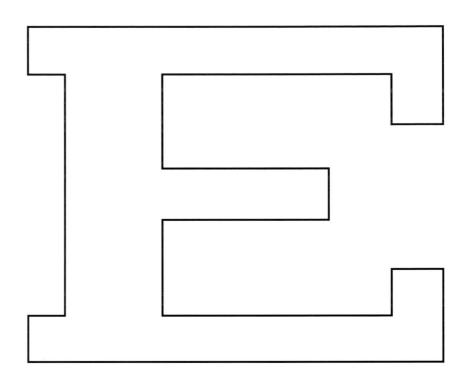

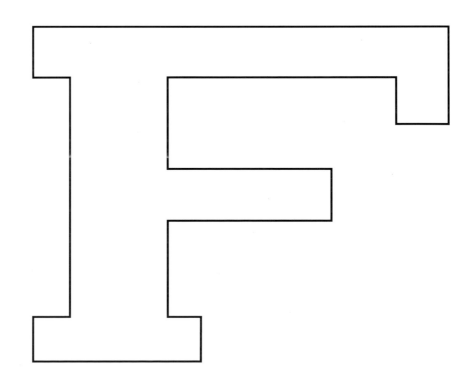

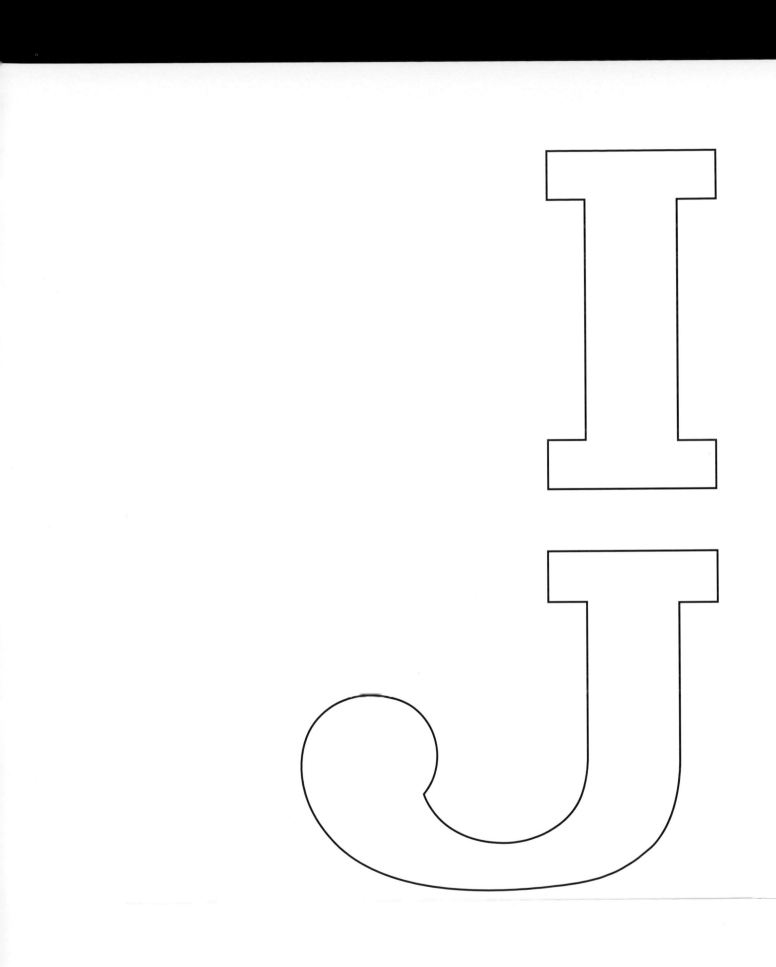

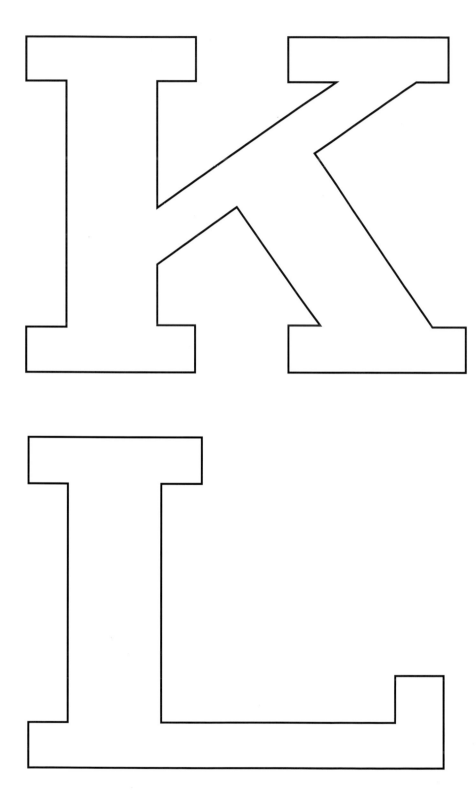

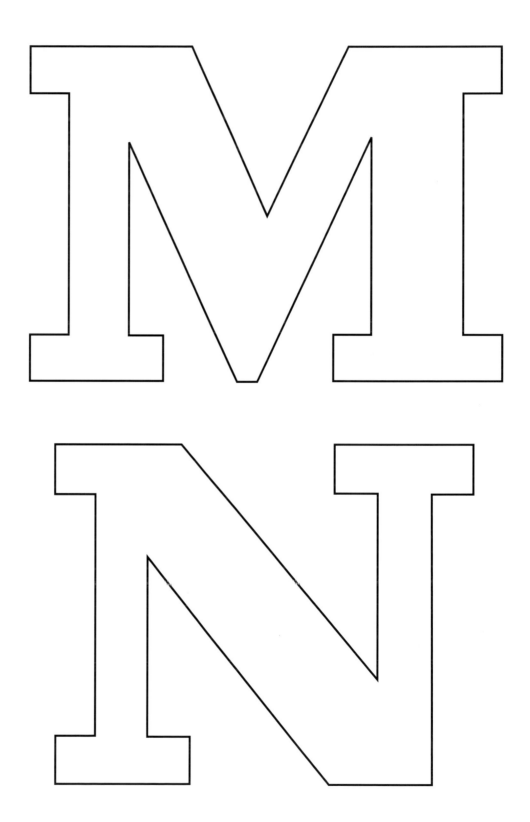

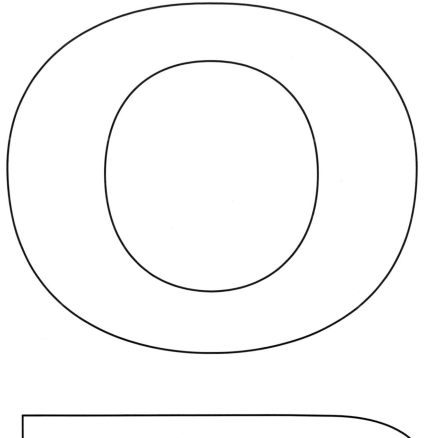

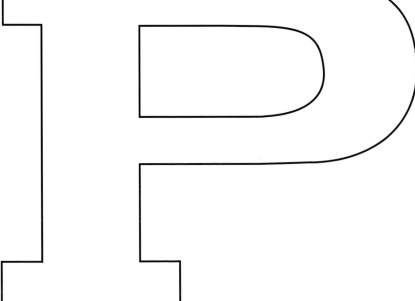

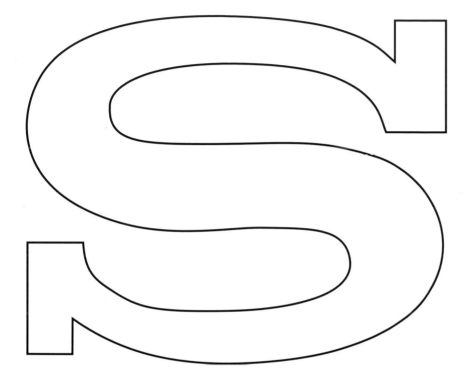

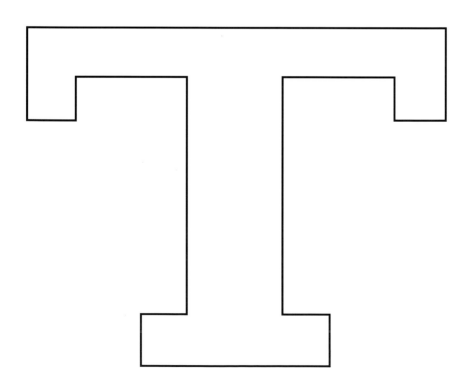

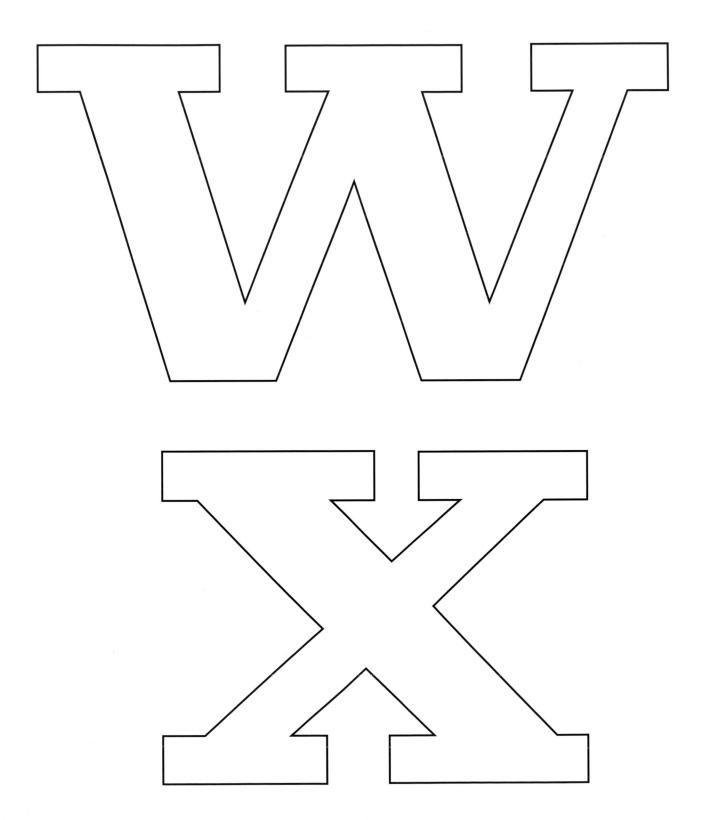

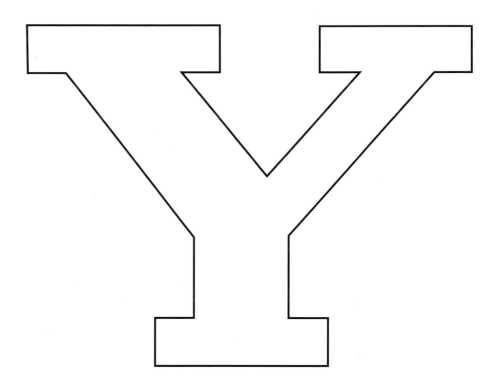

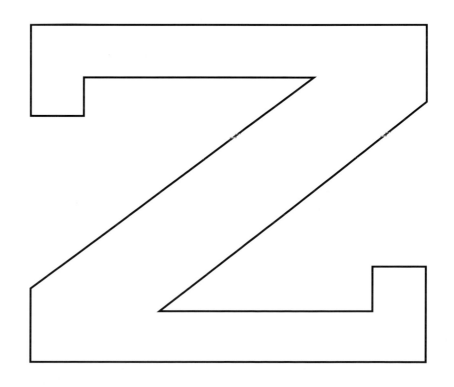

ABOUT THE AUTHOR

Charlotte Patera grew up in Ohio, and worked in Detroit, Chicago, and San Francisco. Her first career was in graphic art, specializing in package design. One of her employers was located on a restored ferryboat docked in San Francisco Bay.

In the late 1960s, Charlotte started a career change by creating distinctive how-to needlecrafts for major magazines including *Better Homes and Gardens* and *Family Circle*. Her interest in appliqué produced an ardent curiosity about the molas of the Kuna Indians of the San Blas Islands in Panama. She sought out accurate mola methods by visiting the San Blas Islands on five occasions—

Photo: C.K. Patera

not as a tourist, but as a needlewoman sharing ideas with the Indian mola makers.

After moving from Marin County, California, to the foothills in the Gold Country of California, Charlotte continues to teach and lecture about her unique methods of appliqué and her Kuna adventures. She has taught around the country and for 10 years at the Houston Quilt Festival. As a change from her sedentary occupation, she can be seen walking the hills in her neighborhood with either classical or global music plugged into her ears. She collects multi-cultural textiles, folk art, and children's books with colorful graphic illustrations.

OTHER FINE BOOKS FROM C&T PUBLISHING:

An Amish Adventure, Roberta Horton
Appliqué 12 Borders and Medallions! Elly Sienkiewicz
Appliqué 12 Easy Ways! Elly Sienkiewicz
The Art of Silk Ribbon Embroidery, Judith Baker Montano
Baltimore Beauties and Beyond (2 Volumes), Elly Sienkiewicz
Beyond the Horizon, Small Landscape Appliqué, Valerie Hearder
Buttonhole Stitch Appliqué, Jean Wells
Colors Changing Hue, Yvonne Porcella
Crazy Quilt Handbook, Judith Montano
Crazy Quilt Odyssey, Judith Montano
Dating Quilts: From 1600 to the Present, A Quick and Easy Reference, Helen Kelley
Dimensional Appliqué—Baskets, Blooms & Baltimore Borders, Elly Sienkiewicz
Elegant Stitches: An Illustrated Stitch Guide & Source Book of Inspiration, Judith Baker Montano
The Fabric Makes the Quilt, Roberta Horton
Faces & Places, Images in Appliqué, Charlotte Warr Andersen
14,287 Pieces of Fabrics and Other Poems, Jean Ray Laury
Friendship's Offering, Susan McKelvey
Heirloom Machine Quilting, Harriet Hargrave
Imagery on Fabric, Jean Ray Laury
Impressionist Quilts, Gai Perry
Isometric Perspective, Katie Pasquini-Masopust
Landscapes & Illusions, Joen Wolfrom
The Magical Effects of Color, Joen Wolfrom

Mariner's Compass, Judy Mathieson
Mariner's Compass Quilts, New Directions, Judy Mathieson
Mastering Machine Appliqué, Harriet Hargrave
Nancy Crow: Improvisational Quilts
Paper Cuts and Plenty, Vol. III of Baltimore Beauties and Beyond, Elly Sienkiewicz
Pattern Play, Doreen Speckmann
Patchwork Quilts Made Easy, Jean Wells (with Rodale Press, Inc.)
Quilts for Fabric Lovers, Alex Anderson
Quilts, Quilts, and More Quilts! Diana McClun and Laura Nownes
Soft-Edge Piecing, Jinny Beyer
Stitching Free: Easy Machine Pictures, Shirley Nilsson
Symmetry: A Design System for Quiltmakers, Ruth B. McDowell
A Treasury of Quilt Labels, Susan McKelvey
Virginia Avery's Hats: A Heady Affair
Virginia Avery's Nifty Neckwear
Visions: Quilts, Layers of Excellence, Quilt San Diego
The Visual Dance: Creating Spectacular Quilts, Joen Wolfrom

For more information write for a free catalog from:
C&T Publishing
P.O. Box 1456
Lafayette, CA 94549
(1-800-284-1114)